LINCOLN AT HOME:

TWO GLIMPSES

OF ABRAHAM LINCOLN'S

DOMESTIC LIFE

ABRAHAM LINCOLN, ABOUT 1846

LINCOLN AT HOME

DAVID HERBERT DONALD

*Two Glimpses of
Abraham Lincoln's
Domestic Life*

WHITE HOUSE HISTORICAL ASSOCIATION
in cooperation with
THORNWILLOW PRESS

1999

WHITE HOUSE HISTORICAL ASSOCIATION
A nonprofit organization, chartered on November 3, 1961, to enhance understanding, appreciation, and enjoyment of the Executive Mansion. Income from the sale of this book will be used to publish other materials about the White House, as well as for the acquisition of historical furnishings and other objects for the Executive Mansion. Address inquiries to 740 Jackson Place, N.W., Washington, D.C. 20503.

This edition of *Lincoln at Home* is reprinted from the handmade, leather-bound volume, published in a limited edition of only 185 copies by the Thornwillow Press.

Library of Congress Catalog Card Number: 99-65023.
ISBN: 0-912308-77-x.

For
Jennifer and Bruce
with love

ACKNOWLEDGMENTS

AN EARLIER VERSION OF "This Damned Old House" appeared in *The White House: The First Two Hundred Years,* edited by Frank Freidel and William Pencak (Boston, 1994), and it is published here through the kind permission of the director of the Northeastern University Press.

Abraham Lincoln's letters to his wife and to his oldest son, Robert, have been published in *The Collected Works of Abraham Lincoln,* edited by Roy P. Basler and others (9 vols.; New Brunswick, 1953–55), and are used here through the courtesy of the Abraham Lincoln Association. Mrs. Lincoln's letters to her husband and son appear in *Mary Todd Lincoln: Her Life and Letters,* edited by Justin C. Turner and Linda Levitt Turner (New York, 1972), and are here published with the permission of Alfred A. Knopf. The letters from Robert Todd Lincoln to his parents are drawn from the Abraham Lincoln Papers in the Library of Congress and, through the kindness of Mr. Kim Bauer, from the Illinois State Historical Library.

INTRODUCTION

MOST OF THE VAST LITERATURE about Abraham Lincoln deals with his public life: his 1858 debates with Stephen A. Douglas, his election to the presidency in 1860, his handling of secession and the Fort Sumter crisis, his management of the huge Union war effort, his Emancipation Proclamation, his triumphant reelection in 1864, his plans for Reconstruction, and his tragic assassination. This emphasis is quite proper, but it is important to remember that Lincoln, during these critical events, also led a private life, defined by his intimate relationship with his wife and by his devotion to their children.

This little book offers two glimpses of Lincoln as a family man. The first section describes the Lincolns' life in the White House during the war years. It originated in a talk I prepared at the request of President George Bush and delivered in the White House on January 7, 1990, as the inaugural lecture in the Presidential Lecture Series. Making it clear that he was in no way trying to restrict my subject matter, the President expressed the hope that I would concentrate on the domestic life of the Lincolns in the White House, in whose history he and Mrs. Bush had such a deep interest.

The assignment could hardly have come at a more opportune moment. I was working on my biography *Lincoln* and was already trying to learn how the Lincoln family lived and fared in Washington. The extensive private tour of the upstairs living quarters of the White House that President and Mrs. Bush gave me just before the lecture was of inestimable value to me in locating the President, his family, and his staff in the Executive Mansion.

(To digress a little, my interest in the domestic life of the Lincolns was further fueled by the warm and generous response of the audience that President and Mrs. Bush had invited to attend the lecture in the great downstairs dining room in the White House. There, beneath the magnificent Healy portrait of Lincoln, the President introduced me to an audience that included, among many others, Chief Justice and Mrs. William Rehnquist, former Chief Justice Warren Burger, General and Mrs. Colin Powell, Secretary and Mrs. Richard

Cheyney, several senators and representatives, some of the leading Lincoln experts and curators, and a number of prominent newspaper and television reporters. Before such an august company my voice was initially a little shaky, but I launched in. Explaining that my topic was not the vast military and political crises of the Lincoln years, but the Lincolns' domestic life, I borrowed a phrase from Allan Nevins that had always amused me and announced that, on this day at least, my muse would soar close to the ground. I went on to say that I brought no lesson to President Bush, no advice on how to govern or how to solve his domestic or foreign problems. At that point, the President, from his front-row seat, audibly blurted out: "Well, he'll be the first one!" That broke the ice, and from that point the lecture went on smoothly.)

That occasion, followed immediately by a splendid reception and a superb exhibit that Mr. Rex Scouten, Curator of the White House, and the White House Historical Association had mounted in the East Room, strengthened my interest in the Lincolns' family life and led to the compilation of the second part of the present book: a collection of all the known letters exchanged by Abraham and Mary Lincoln and their children. Most of these letters—though not all—have long been available to historians and biographers, but they have been published in a scattered fashion. Lincoln's letters to his wife and family appear in the nine volumes of his *Collected Works,* interspersed among letters and messages dealing with all manner of political and legal matters. Mary Lincoln's letters to her husband and to her oldest son, Robert Todd Lincoln, are published in a large volume containing all her correspondence. Nobody has collected Robert's letters. By bringing these letters together, I wanted to present a picture of the Lincolns' domestic life. They offer a portrait of Mrs. Lincoln unmarred by tittle-tattle and by later gossip, and they show Abraham Lincoln as a devoted, if often desperately busy and distracted, family man.

D H D

LINCOLN AT HOME:
TWO GLIMPSES
OF ABRAHAM LINCOLN'S
DOMESTIC LIFE

PART I

"THIS DAMNED OLD HOUSE":
THE LINCOLNS
IN THE WHITE HOUSE

MARY TODD LINCOLN, ABOUT 1846

PART I

"THIS DAMNED OLD HOUSE":
THE LINCOLNS
IN THE WHITE HOUSE

SHORTLY after Abraham Lincoln was inaugurated president in 1861, an old friend from Illinois asked him how he liked living in the Executive Mansion (as the White House was generally called in those days). Lincoln replied that he felt a bit like the reprobate in Springfield who had been tarred and feathered and ridden out of town on a rail. If it wasn't for the honor of it, he said, he'd much rather have walked.[1] That wry, detached attitude was to serve Lincoln well during his four years in the White House. It was, unfortunately, not an attitude that his wife, Mary Todd Lincoln, could share.

I

When the Lincolns moved into the White House on March 4, 1861, they were less prepared than any previous occupants for the duties and challenges they would have to face. An able Illinois lawyer who had gained a national reputation in his debates with Stephen A. Douglas, Lincoln, at the age of fifty-two, had no administrative experience of any sort; he had never been governor of his state or even mayor of his town of Springfield. A profound student of the Constitution and of the writings of the Founding Fathers, he had a limited acquaintance with the government that they had established. He had served only a single, rather unsuccessful term in the House of Representatives in the 1840s and had not returned to the national capital since. Though Lincoln was one of the founders of the Republican party, he had few acquaintances and almost no close personal friends in Washington. In charge of the country's foreign relations, he had no correspondents abroad and no acquaintance with any ruler of a foreign nation.

Nearly a decade younger than her husband, Mary Lincoln was equally unprepared to be mistress of the White House. The daughter of a well-to-do merchant and cotton manufacturer, she had grown up in comfort in Lexington, Kentucky, where she had received the best education available for young women—including instruction in French. But for the previous twenty-five years, she had lived in semi-frontier Illinois, with only an occasional visit to her Kentucky relatives and one unhappy winter in Washington when her husband was in Congress. In a modest frame house on Eighth Street in Springfield, she had made a comfortable middle-class home for her husband and their children. Like her husband, she had no friends in Washington.

Clearly, had the Lincolns occupied the Executive Mansion during the most tranquil of times they would have faced difficulties. But in 1861 the circumstances were particularly trying. The states of the Deep South had seceded and set up the Confederate States of America. While Confederate troops besieged Fort Sumter in Charleston Harbor, one of the few installations in the South still in Union hands, the states of the Upper South teetered between union and secession. Lincoln had to face this crisis as the first Republican president, obliged to create an administration from discordant groups that had never before worked together. Even as Lincoln was sworn into office, members of his party were beating on the doors of the White House demanding that the spoils of office be distributed to the party faithful. Hounded by office seekers, Lincoln said he sometimes felt like a hotel keeper who was trying to put out a fire in one wing of his establishment while renting rooms in another.

Mary Lincoln's problems were equally severe. Because she was the wife of a Republican—who completely supported her husband's views and ambitions—the Southern women who dominated Washington society resolved to snub her. The few New England women in the national capital distrusted her because she was Southern-born and because, eventually, four of her brothers and three of her brothers-in-law enlisted in the Confederate army. Easterners in general were sure that she was an uncouth frontier woman—doubtless as uneducated as an Indian squaw, and smoking a corncob pipe. Whatever she did—or failed to do—was certain to be closely watched and criticized.

It was, then, with trepidation that the Lincolns on the morning after the inauguration began to explore the Executive Mansion. They were overwhelmed by the size of their new residence with its thirty-one rooms, not including the conservatory, various outbuildings, and stables. The East Room alone was about as large as their entire Springfield house. After a quick inspection, Lincoln, who was totally indifferent to his physical surroundings, concluded that the mansion was in good shape, and was ready to settle down to work. But Mrs. Lincoln came up with a very different verdict. Accompanied by her sisters, who were visiting her from Springfield, she went from room to room, finding the furniture broken down, the wallpaper peeling, the carpeting worn, the draperies torn, the eleven basement rooms filthy and rat-infested; the whole place had the air of a run-down, unsuccessful, third-rate hotel.[2]

Both the Lincolns promptly discovered that the Executive Mansion was as much a public building as it was a home. Except for the family dining rooms, all the rooms on the first floor were open to all visitors, and anybody who wanted to could stroll in at any hour of the day and often late at night. A single elderly doorkeeper was supposed to prevent depredations, but often no one was on duty.[3]

On the second floor, nearly half of the rooms were also public; they were devoted to the business of the chief executive. Here were a reception room, the offices of the president's secretary, and the president's own office, which also served as the cabinet room. A solid black walnut table occupied the center of the president's office. Along one wall of the room were a sofa and two upholstered chairs, above which hung maps of the theaters of military operations. In a corner by the window was a large upright mahogany desk, so battered that one of Lincoln's secretaries thought it must have come "from some old furniture auction"; the pigeonholes above it served as a filing cabinet. Lincoln's smaller working desk stood between the two windows.[4] All the furnishings of this wing of the White House were of the most nondescript kind, and the floor was mostly covered with oil-cloth, which made it easier to clean up after overflowing or missed spittoons.

From early morning until dusk, these rooms were thronged with senators, congressmen, applicants for government jobs, candidates for military appointments, foreign dignitaries, and plain citizens who had favors to ask or who just wanted to shake their president's hand. In the early months of Lincoln's first administration, the line was often so long that it extended down the stairs to the front entrance, with a candidate for a job or a military appointment perched on each step. Lincoln found himself a prisoner in his own office; every time he stepped out into the corridor to go to the family quarters on the west end of the building, he was besieged with complaints and petitions. Finally, in order to gain a little privacy, he ordered the only structural addition made to the White House during his administration—a partition built through the reception room, which allowed him to retreat unobserved from his office into the family's private rooms.

Those private quarters, which initially seemed so palatial, proved to be remarkably constricted. There were, in fact, only six or seven rooms where the Lincolns could enjoy any privacy. They made the upstairs oval room the family sitting room. The two adjoining rooms on the south side were those of President and Mrs. Lincoln; as in Springfield, they used separate, but connecting, bedrooms. Across the wide corridor were the "Prince of Wales Room," the state guest room of the Executive Mansion, and the infrequently used room of their oldest son, Robert Todd Lincoln, a student at Harvard College, who was in the White House only during brief vacation periods; the rest of the time it served as a guest room.[5] Also on the north side were the rooms of the two youngest Lincoln boys—Willie, aged ten, and Thomas (always called "Tad"), who was eight.

II

The two younger Lincoln boys found endless opportunities for adventure and mischief in the Executive Mansion. Adults saw the soldiers stationed on the south grounds of the White House as an ominous reminder of danger, but to Willie and Tad the members of the "Bucktail" Pennsylvania regiment were playmates who could always be counted on for stories and races. Catching the martial spirit, Willie and Tad took great pleasure in drilling all the neighborhood boys they could round up. With two special friends who just matched them in age—Bud and Holly Taft, children of a federal judge who lived nearby—they commandeered the roof of the mansion for their fort, and here, with small logs painted to look like cannon, they resolutely fired away at unseen Confederates across the Potomac. Intensely patriotic, Willie published a poem in the Washington *National Republican* about the heroic death of a friend at Ball's Bluff. Tad, a little less clear about what was going on, managed to create a sensation when his father was solemnly reviewing Union troops on Pennsylvania Avenue by slipping in behind the president and waving a Confederate flag.[6]

Children in the White House were something new for Americans, and citizens began showering them with presents. The most valued, and the most lasting, were the pets. Someone presented to Willie a beautiful little pony, to which he was devoted; he rode the animal nearly every day and, being a generous boy, often allowed Tad to ride, even though the younger boy was so small that his legs stuck straight out on the sides. Especially cherished were two small goats, Nanko and Nannie, which frisked on the White House grounds and, when they had an opportunity, wrought destruction in the White House garden. But they were not entirely outside animals; like the public at large, they had the run of the White House. On one occasion Tad harnessed Nanko up to a chair, which served as a sled, and drove triumphantly through the East Room, where a reception was in progress. As dignified matrons held up their hoop skirts, Nanko pulled the yelling boy around the room and out through the door again.[7]

When Lincoln could, he played with his boys.

One day Julia Taft, the teen-aged sister of Bud and Holly, heard a great commotion in the upstairs oval room and, entering, found the president of the United States lying on his back on the floor, Willie and Bud holding down his arms, Tad and Holly, his legs. "Julie, come quick and sit on his stomach!" cried Tad, as the president grinned at her grandly. There were also quiet times, when Lincoln told stories or read to the boys; he would balance Willie and Bud on each knee, while Tad mounted on the back of his big chair and Holly climbed on the arm.[8]

But during his first year in office, Lincoln had all too little time for his sons, for he was busy learning his job. The Department of State sent over a detailed memorandum of the clothing that a president was expected to wear. Obediently, Lincoln followed directions, though, with his ungainly figure and his immense height, his coat always seemed rumpled and his cravat askew. His huge hands, enlarged by years of plowing and splitting rails, were never comfortable in the white kid gloves that the State Department prescribed; once, holding up his hands encased in a new pair of these gloves, he said they looked like canvassed hams.

In the first days of his administration he tried to be orderly and businesslike. For instance, he began by trying to scan and digest all the morning papers that reached the White House. Finding that too time-consuming, he instructed his secretaries to prepare a digest of the news for his perusal, but presently he discontinued even that. Though occasionally he glanced at the telegraphic news despatches in one or two papers, he read none of the papers consistently and almost never looked at their editorials. There was, he concluded, nothing that newspapermen could tell him that he did not already know.

After the early days of the administration, much of Lincoln's mail received no closer attention than did the newspapers. To assist the chief executive, the Congress had provided a staff of only one secretary. Since even the methodical young German, John G. Nicolay, whom Lincoln appointed to this office, could not begin to handle all the work, the president was allowed, in effect, to borrow two additional clerks from other offices of the government.[9] A principal duty of these three young men was to screen the president's mail—some two hundred or three hundred letters a day. Scores of these were requests for information or applications for jobs that could readily be referred to the cabinet departments. Dozens of other letters they simply threw into the wastebasket: crank letters, threatening letters, letters containing messages from supernatural powers, letters soliciting the president's endorsement of commercial schemes. The rest, which the secretaries carefully endorsed on the back with the name of the writer and a brief indication of the contents, had to be seen and answered by the president himself. To many of these he replied in his own handwriting, often taking the time to make a careful copy of his response for his files. Then letters and answers were filed away in the pigeonholes above the president's desk.

Lincoln worked long hours at his desk. Much of his time was taken in receiving the hundreds of candidates, applicants, petitioners, suppliants, and visitors who wanted to see him. Most of these he handled expeditiously, quickly scanning letters of recommendation and referring them to the proper authorities, listening intently to complaints and

16

making proper sympathetic noises. Whenever possible he avoided flatly rejecting an application for help, preferring to tell one of his celebrated "leetle stories" to suggest the unreasonableness of the request. For instance, when an officer accused of embezzling forty dollars of government money appealed for leniency on the ground that he had really stolen only thirty dollars, Lincoln was reminded of an Indiana man who charged his neighbor's daughter with unseemly behavior for having three illegitimate children. "'Now,' said the man whose family was so outrageously scandalized, 'that's a lie, and I can prove it, for she only has two.'"[10]

Lincoln's friends worried that he was confined to his office so much of the time and urged him to get fresh air and take exercise, but the president insisted upon seeing everybody who wanted to see him. "They do not want much, and they get very little," he said. "I know how I would feel in their place."[11]

Remarkably, during Lincoln's first year in office, the president's systematic lack of system seemed to work. Stories of his patience, his humanity, his accessibility to even the humblest petitioner spread throughout the North. Millions referred to him as Father Abraham—though, in fact, he was one of the youngest men elected president. For the first time in American history, citizens began to feel that the occupant of the White House was *their* representative, and they showered him with gifts: a firkin of butter, a crate of Bartlett pears, New England salmon. With special appropriateness a man from Johnsburgh, New York, sent Lincoln "a live American Eagle[,] the bird of our land," which had lost one foot in a trap. "But," the New Yorker continued, "he is yet an Eagle and perhaps no more cripled [*sic*] than the Nation whose banner he represented; his wings are sound and will extend seven feet."[12]

In part the common people rallied behind the new president because, in time of war, most Americans support their government. They were content to give the new administration a chance to find itself. Even the disaster to Union troops at the battle of Bull Run in July 1861 did little to abate this willingness. And by the beginning of 1862 it appeared that the Lincoln government was beginning to be master of the situation. In the West,

General Ulysses S. Grant broke the Confederate line at Forts Henry and Donelson and most of Tennessee fell into Union hands. In the South, Commodore David G. Farragut captured New Orleans. On the seaboard, Union amphibious teams established a foothold on the Sea Islands of South Carolina and had control of Cape Hatteras in North Carolina. And in the East, General George B. McClellan had recruited, organized, and drilled the finest army ever seen on the American continent, which seemed poised to capture Richmond. It was little wonder that by early spring Lincoln's mail was filled with letters like one from retired General Winfield Scott rejoicing in "the inevitable and early suppression of the Great American rebellion."[13]

Meanwhile, during these same twelve months, Mrs. Lincoln was achieving some successes of her own. Indeed, she became the most conspicuous female occupant of the Executive Mansion since Dolley Madison. Brought up to express an active interest in public affairs, deeply involved in her husband's political career, Mary Lincoln had no intention of fading quietly into the background in

Washington. She intended to become, and was, the First Lady of the land—a term that was coined to describe her.

She made it her main project to refurbish the White House. Congress had appropriated $20,000 to be expended over the four years of her husband's term of office for the rehabilitation of the Executive Mansion. This was, to her, an immense amount of money—worth at least ten times as much in present-day purchasing power; it was more than four times the Lincoln family's total income in the average year before 1860. To Mary it seemed an infinite treasure.

She went to New York and Philadelphia in order to buy furnishings suitable for the mansion of the president of the United States and his First Lady. Merchants welcomed her with open arms, showing her the best and most expensive carpeting, material for upholstery and drapes, furniture, and china. She bought everything. Much of her effort went into making the upstairs living quarters homey and comfortable. She took special pains with the guest bedroom, repapering it with light purple wallpaper figured with gold roses. For this room she ordered the ornately carved seven-foot rosewood bed that has since been known as the "Lincoln bed," though in fact the president probably never slept in it. It was framed in the most elegant of canopies, made of purple silk trimmed with gold lace gathered together at the headboard in a gold coronet. But most of her purchases were for the public rooms downstairs. The receipted bills in the National Archives show that she purchased chairs, sofas, and hassocks; fabrics of damask, brocade, pink tarlatan, plush, and "French Satin DeLaine"; wallpaper imported from France; and a full set of Haviland china in "Solferino and gold," with the American coat of arms in the center of each plate. For the Red Room she ordered 117 yards of crimson Wilton carpet; and for the East Room, an imported Brussels velvet carpet, pale green in color, ingeniously woven as a single piece,[14] which, one admirer gushed, "in effect looked as if the ocean, in gleaming and transparent waves, were tossing roses at your feet."[15]

Returning to Washington, she personally oversaw the scrubbing, painting, and plastering of the entire White House, so that for the first time in years the Executive Mansion was sparklingly clean. As her new furnishings began to arrive, the whole place took on a look of elegance. To modern eyes Mary Lincoln's fondness for ornate laces, for heavy, tasseled drapes, for plush, overstuffed furniture seems at best quaint and at worst vulgar; but this was the height of the Victorian age, when less was certainly not more. Even critical observers were impressed by her accomplishment.

But then, inevitably, the bills began coming in. In December 1861 she discovered that she had exceeded the congressional appropriation by $6,700. She sought desperately to hide her extravagance from her husband, arguing—quite correctly—that such overruns were common in governmental expenditures and that this deficit could easily be concealed by a little budget-juggling. Finally, she was obliged to ask the Commissioner of Public Buildings, who kept the White House accounts, to explain the situation to the president and to ask him to sponsor a supplemental congressional appropriation.

Lincoln was furious. He would never, he said, endorse such a deficiency appropriation. "It would stink in the nostrils of the American people to have it said that the President of the United States had approved a bill overrunning an appropriation of $20,000 for *flub dubs* for this damned old house, when the soldiers cannot have blankets." "It was all wrong to spend one cent at such a time," he went on, "and I never ought to have had a cent expended; the house was furnished well enough, better than any one we ever lived in."[16] Rather than ask Congress for more money, he vowed to pay for Mary's purchases out of his own pocket. Eventually, though, he was obliged to recede from his position, and Congress quietly passed two deficiency appropriations to cover Mary Lincoln's expenditures.

With that obstacle overcome, Mary Lincoln was ready to celebrate her success, and on February 5, 1862, she held a reception, with admission limited to five hundred invited guests, rather than being open to the public at large. Inevitably, there was much grumbling among those who were not invited. Carriages began arriving about nine in the evening with besworded, overdecorated diplomats, generals in bright uniforms, members of the cabinet, Supreme Court justices, and selected senators and congressmen. In the East Room they were greeted by the president, who was wearing a black swallowtail coat, and the First Lady, whose white silk dress, decorated with hundreds of small black flowers, exposed a remarkably low décolletage. In the background the United States Marine Band played, its repertoire including a sprightly new piece, "The Mary Lincoln Polka." At midnight the doors to the dining room were opened to reveal a magnificent buffet concocted by Maillard's of New York, which displayed sugary models of the Ship of State, Fort Sumter, and Fort Pickens flanked by mounds of turkey, duck, ham, terrapin, and pheasant. Dinner was served until three, and many guests stayed till daybreak. Altogether, concluded the *Washington Star*, the reception was "the most superb affair of its kind ever seen here."[17]

III

That February 1862 party marked a turning point in the Lincolns' life in the White House. Even while the visitors downstairs were celebrating Mary Lincoln's refurbishing of the Executive Mansion and Abraham Lincoln's prospective victory over the Confederacy, upstairs the two small Lincoln boys were desperately ill with "bilious fever"—probably typhoid fever, caused by pollution in the White House water system. Deeply anxious, their parents had considered canceling the grand reception, but the family doctor assured them that the boys were in no immediate danger. Even so, both the president and his wife quietly slipped upstairs during the celebration to be at their sons' bedsides. During the next two weeks, Tad continued to be very ill, but Willie grew worse and worse. On Thursday, February 20, he died.

Both parents were prostrated with grief. Lincoln had loved this cheerful, intelligent boy probably more than any of his other children, and he found it difficult to accept his loss. Though he had to go through the motions of continuing the business of the presidency, his heart was not in it. But slowly he came to identify the loss of Willie with that of so many other young Americans who were dying from disease or battle, and his private grief became the source for an even greater resolution to preserve the Union.

His wife could not so sublimate her grief. Having earlier lost a favorite son, Eddie, in Springfield, Mary Lincoln could not deal with this second death, and for three weeks she took to her bed, so desolated that she could not attend the funeral or look after Tad, who was slowly beginning to recover. For many months the mere mention of Willie's name was enough to send her into paroxysms of weeping, and it was necessary for Lincoln to employ a nurse to look after her. Never again did Mary Lincoln enter the bedroom where Willie had died, nor the downstairs Green Room, where his body had been embalmed. When she was finally able to emerge from her room, Mary Lincoln went into such profound mourning dress that she was almost invisible under the layers of black veils and crepes.

In these circumstances, of course, all social activities at the White House ceased, as the Executive Mansion was heavily draped in black. Grieving over the death of her son, Mary Lincoln gave little further thought to the mansion that she had so tastefully redecorated, and in the months following Willie's death, while the public rooms were largely unattended and unoccupied, an enormous amount of vandalism occurred. Souvenir hunters managed to steal yard-long swatches of the drapes and carpets and to cut out the delicate medallions from the lace curtains.

But such material concerns were no longer of much interest to Mary Lincoln, who sought to reach out to Willie beyond the grave. Presently she became the victim of spiritualists, who claimed they could put her in touch with her darling lost boy. Often she went to a medium's darkened chambers, but on eight occasions séances were held in the White House itself. The president attended at least one of these, not out of any belief in spiritualism, but in a desire to see who was preying on his wife's mental instability.[18]

It would, however, have been difficult to blame President Lincoln had he sought any kind of supernatural help at this time, since his own successes seemed as transient as Mary Lincoln's. By mid-1862 it was clear that the anticipated Union victory in the Civil War was not coming about. In the western theater, after the bloody battle of Shiloh, the Union armies were stalled. In the East, the Army of the Potomac got within sight of Richmond but then was driven back. With his grand strategy crumbling, Lincoln desperately sought new commanders who could bring quick victories. In a game of military musical chairs, General John Pope took command and brought about the

Union defeat at Second Bull Run; Ambrose P. Burnside led in the fiasco at Fredericksburg; boastful Joseph Hooker brought about the rout at Chancellorsville. With military defeats came political rebuffs. Invoking military necessity, Lincoln issued his Emancipation Proclamation, which contributed to the defeat of the Republican party in the congressional elections of 1862. So inept was Lincoln thought to be that in December 1862 a caucus of the leaders of his own party in the Senate urged him to fire his secretary of state and reconstruct his whole cabinet.

Though shaken, the president applied himself to the duties of his office with a grim intensity that helped distract him from his personal woes. Rising early after a generally sleepless night, Lincoln went at once to his desk, where he worked for an hour or so before breakfast, which consisted of a cup of coffee and an egg. He returned to his office to examine papers and sign commissions for another hour or so until ten o'clock, when public petitioners were allowed in. At one o'clock—unless he forgot about it—he took a brief break for lunch with Mary and Tad and occasionally a close family friend; abstemious as always, he customarily ate only an apple and drank a glass of milk. Then he went back to the office, where he remained for most of the afternoon, unless he could be persuaded to take a horseback or carriage ride. Having no interest in food, he ate a spartan dinner, with no alcohol, and unless there was some ceremony or reception that required his presence, he once again went back to his desk. Late at night he would frequently walk alone through the White House grounds to the War Department to read the latest telegraphic despatches from the armies. Only then, if there was no major fighting underway, did he feel he could relax for a few minutes with his family. "I consider myself fortunate," Mary Lincoln wrote at this time, "if at eleven o'clock, I once more find myself, in my pleasant room and very especially, if my tired and weary Husband is *there*, waiting in the lounge to receive me."[19]

Inevitably, with such a schedule, President and Mrs. Lincoln began to drift apart. For some time the Lincolns had slept in separate, but adjoining, bedrooms; now, after the death of Willie, Tad was so lonely and so subject to nightmares that he was regularly allowed to sleep in his father's bed.

Mary Lincoln was totally absorbed in her own affairs and in her grief. Lincoln, of course, was aware of his wife's unstable condition, but nobody knew how such mental illness should be treated. In any case, he was desperately exhausted. Always thin, he had now lost so much weight as to look cadaverous. Though worn out, he managed to keep his sense of humor about his appearance; when somebody told him he was "thin as a shad," he responded—in an atrocious pun—that he looked even "worse—as thin as a shadder."[20] Great black circles ringed his eyes. Chronically weary, he was never able to get any rest; as he expressed it, the little relaxation he allowed himself "seemed never to reach the *tired* spot."[21]

Coming to regard the White House as a prison, both the Lincolns were happy to escape during the summer months to a cottage on the grounds of the Soldiers' Home, three miles north of Washington. But presidential duties continued without interruption, and Lincoln rode or drove back and forth to his office every day. Nor did Mary Lincoln's anxieties abate. She was often in a state of near-hysteria concerning her husband's safety—and with reason, because on one occasion when Lincoln was riding to the White House, a stray bullet, whether from a would-be assassin or an overzealous soldier, penetrated his hat. Mary had an additional source of worry because her oldest son, Robert, about to graduate from Harvard, wanted to enlist in the Union army. He had the tacit approval of his father, but she frantically and obdurately opposed it, saying that she had already sacrificed one son to the Union cause and could not spare another.

IV

A year after Willie's death, Mary Lincoln emerged from full mourning, and the endless round of White House entertainment began again. Hardly a week passed without one or two state dinners at the White House—for the diplomatic corps, for visiting foreign dignitaries, for congressmen. Every week there were two evening receptions, one on Tuesday and the other on Saturday. At eight o'clock guests were admitted at the North Portico and crossed the broad corridor to the Red Room. There the master of ceremonies —usually Ward Hill Lamon, an old Illinois friend who was now marshal of the District of Columbia —introduced them to the president, who shook each guest's hand, even though by the end of one of these evenings his own hands were usually raw with blisters. They were then presented to Mrs. Lincoln, who was saved from having to shake hands because her hoop skirts made it impossible for anyone to approach closer than three feet. They were next shepherded through the Green Room into the great East Room, where they stood about and talked; no food or drink was served. At ten o'clock the president, with Mrs. Lincoln on his arm, entered and made a circuit of the room, the U.S. Marine Band played "Hail Columbia," and the party was over.[22]

These social affairs were exhausting to the tired president and his distraught wife. Bored and depressed, the Lincolns were not at their best on these occasions. Coming away from a reception, Richard Henry Dana, Jr., reported that "Mrs. Lincoln looks like the housekeeper of the establishment, and a notable, prying and not goodtempered housekeeper," while "'Abe' looks like a man who has brought in something to sell."[23] Aware of such criticisms, both Lincolns believed such social functions were necessary to maintain morale in time of war. Anyway, the president claimed these thousands of visitors were valuable to him; they gave him a "public opinion bath," a better way of understanding what ordinary citizens were thinking and saying.

By this time Mary Lincoln had largely abandoned her efforts to impress Washington society, and she now devoted her limited energy to visiting the wounded Union soldiers in the army hospitals around Washington, bringing them flowers from the White House conservatory and offering comfort and advice. She also took a special interest in the camps of "contrabands," former slaves who had congregated in the District of Columbia, often without housing, food, or elementary medical facilities. Unfortunately for her reputation, she failed to take a friendly newspaper correspondent or two along with her on these expeditions of mercy, and they went largely unnoticed by a public daily made aware of her increasingly eccentric behavior.

She began to travel a good deal, usually accompanied by Tad. There were trips to New York, to Long Branch, New Jersey, to Boston to see Robert, and to the White Mountains. And everywhere she went, she gratified her passion for shopping;

once directed toward refitting the White House, it was now indulged to outfit her person. She could not check her desire to buy; she needed a $1,500 cashmere shawl, she needed new dresses, she needed specially made hats, she needed gloves— indeed, it was said that she purchased no fewer than four hundred pairs of gloves in a three-month period. Her passion for material possessions became boundless. When the Lincoln family —all three members—moved to the Soldiers' Home for the summer of 1863, she required a train of nineteen wagons to haul out the necessary supplies and clothing.

Though Mary Lincoln was not by this point entirely rational, there was a kind of logic—to be sure, a circular logic—behind her obsessive concern for clothing. She knew that she was accumulating huge debts, but she thought a failure to dress in proper style would cause people to turn against her husband and result in his defeat in the 1864 presidential election. "If he is re-elected, I can keep him in ignorance of my affairs," she thought, "but if he is defeated, then the bills will be sent in, and he will know all."[24]

Though proud of his wife's handsome appearance, the president, it is certain, never thought of Mary Lincoln's expensive dresses as a factor in his reelection. Much more important in his mind was the continued failure of the Union armies to achieve victory on the battlefield. In mid-1863 Union successes at Vicksburg and Gettysburg roused Northern hopes, but neither victory was followed by further decisive action. The following year Grant, brought East as commander in chief of all the Union armies, led a series of direct assaults on Confederate armies which by mid-year brought him no closer to Richmond than McClellan had been two years earlier. War-weariness among civilians and desertion among soldiers were rampant, and the Democrats nominated General McClellan for president on a platform that promised peace. So dispiriting was the outlook that Lincoln glumly predicted his own defeat in the 1864 election.

Then the tide turned. General William T. Sherman's capture of Atlanta came just in time to cheer Union supporters throughout the North, and Lincoln was reelected. Shortly afterward, as Sherman blazed a track of destruction across Georgia and Grant gained a stranglehold on

Richmond, it became clear that the Confederacy was doomed. Night after night the White House was illuminated to celebrate Union victories, and crowds gathered on the North Lawn to serenade the president and to hear a few words from him about the successes Union arms were achieving.

Life in the White House during these final weeks of the conflict achieved a tranquillity that the Lincolns had not hitherto known. With all the major decisions made, with the armies admirably commanded, the president no longer had to feel personally responsible for every action or to sit up nights waiting in the telegraph room of the War Department for news of the latest disaster. Aware that there were still severe political problems, he tried to get some rest. He made a point of taking Mary and Tad on several little jaunts, ostensibly to inspect the armies, but in fact to secure a respite from his daily routine.

As the end of the war approached, both Lincolns felt they were awakening from what Mary called "this hideous nightmare" through which they had been living. On Friday, April 14, 1865, the president seemed particularly happy. "Dear husband," Mary remarked, "you almost startle me, by your great cheerfulness." That afternoon they took a carriage ride, and the president, "cheerful — . . . even playful," talked of the happier times ahead of them. "Mary," he said, "I consider *this day*, the war has come to a close.—We must *both*, be more cheerful in the future—between the war & the loss of our darling Willie—we have both, been very miserable."[25] By the time they returned to the White House, Mary was beginning to have one of her headaches and thought of staying at home for the evening. But Lincoln had already given his word that he would appear in the presidential box at the popular Ford's Theatre. Mary put on a pretty bonnet and a small-patterned blue dress, and he got ready by brushing his hair with his hand and picking up his silk hat. Arm in arm they went out the north door of the White House for the last time together.

NOTES

1. J. G. Randall, *Lincoln the President: Midstream* (New York: Dodd, Mead & Co., 1952), 2.

2. For a full and valuable account of the Lincolns in the White House, see William Seale, *The President's House: A History* (Washington: White House Historical Association, 1986), chaps. 15–17.

3. On White House security, see William A. Croffut, "Lincoln's Washington: Recollections of a Journalist Who Knew Everybody," *Atlantic Monthly* 145 (January 1930): 64.

4. William O. Stoddard, *Inside the White House in War Times* (New York: Charles L. Webster & Co., 1890), 23–24. Cf. the drawing C. L. Stellwagen made of Lincoln's office in October 1864, in White House Historical Association, *The White House: An Historical Guide* (Washington: White House Historical Association, 1963), 128.

5. For a diagram showing the public and private rooms on the second floor, see Seale, *The President's House*, 394 ff.

6. For an engaging account of the Lincoln children in the White House, see Ruth Painter Randall, *Lincoln's Sons* (Boston: Little, Brown & Co., 1955).

7. On the pets in the Lincoln household, see Ruth Paintter Randall, *Lincoln's Animal Friends* (Boston: Little, Brown & Co., 1958).

8. Julia Taft Bayne, *Tad Lincoln's Father* (Boston: Little, Brown & Co., 1931), 108, 110.

9. On Nicolay and the administration of the president's office, see Helen Nicolay, *Lincoln's Secretary: A Biography of John G. Nicolay* (New York: Longmans, Green and Co., 1949). See also Edward D. Neill, *Abraham Lincoln and His Mailbag* (St. Paul: Minnesota Historical Society, 1964), 46–50.

10. Ward Hill Lamon, *Recollections of Abraham Lincoln, 1847–1865*, ed. Dorothy Lamon Teillard (Washington, 1911), 82–83.

11. Benjamin P. Thomas, *Abraham Lincoln: A Biography* (New York: Alfred A. Knopf, 1952), 457.

12. D. M. Jenks to Abraham Lincoln, June 10, 1862, Abraham Lincoln Manuscripts, Library of Congress.

13. Winfield Scott to W. H. Seward, April 28, 1862, Lincoln MSS.

14. On these purchases, see Ruth Painter Randall, *Mary Lincoln: Biography of a Marriage* (Boston: Little, Brown & Co., 1953), 260–61.

15. Mary Clemmer Ames, *Ten Years in Washington* (Hartford, Conn.: A. D. Worthington & Co., 1873), 171–72.

16. Ruth P. Randall, *Mary Lincoln*, 264–65. Cf. Benjamin Brown French, *Witness to the Young Republic*, ed. Donald B. Cole and John J. McDonough (Hanover, N.H.: University Press of New England, 1989), 382.

17. For an elaborate account of this reception, together with a wood engraving of the scene, see *Frank Leslie's Illustrated Newspaper* 13 (February 22, 1862): 209–10, 213–14. Marie D. Smith, *Entertaining in the White House* (Washington: Acropolis Books, 1967), 102, gives the menu.

18. For a sympathetic presentation of Mary Lincoln's interest in spiritualism, see Jean Harvey Baker, *Mary Todd Lincoln: A Biography* (New York: W. W. Norton & Co., 1987), 214–22.

19. Justin G. Turner and Linda Levitt Turner, *Mary Todd Lincoln: Her Life and Letters* (New York: Alfred A. Knopf, 1972), 187.

20. J. G. Randall, *Lincoln the President: Midstream*, 64.

21. Francis B. Carpenter, *The Inner Life of Abraham Lincoln: Six Months at the White House* (Boston: Houghton, Osgood and Co., 1879), 217.

22. Stoddard, *Inside the White House*, 96–97.

23. Richard Henry Dana, Jr., Diary, January 7, 1862, Dana Manuscripts, Massachusetts Historical Society.

24. Elizabeth Keckley, *Behind the Scenes: Thirty Years a Slave and Four Years in the White House* (New York: Arno Press, 1968), 150.

25. Carl Sandburg and Paul M. Angle, *Mary Lincoln: Wife and Widow* (New York: Harcourt & Co., 1932), 242.

PART II

FAMILY LETTERS:
THE LETTERS OF ABRAHAM LINCOLN,
MARY TODD LINCOLN
AND
ROBERT TODD LINCOLN
1848–1865

LINCOLN AND TAD, 1864

PART II

FAMILY LETTERS:
THE LETTERS OF ABRAHAM LINCOLN,
MARY TODD LINCOLN
AND
ROBERT TODD LINCOLN
1848–1865

ABRAHAM AND MARY LINCOLN did not ex-
change a great many letters because for most of
their married life they lived under the same roof,
and not all of the letters they did write have been
preserved. But the letters that have survived offer
an intimate view of the Lincoln family. These are
not letters of passionate young people in love, for
by 1848, the date of the first surviving letter, the
Lincolns had been married for six years and already had two children, but they show an affec-
tionate couple who were often lonely and unhappy
when they were obliged to be apart. In their letters Lincoln and his wife exchanged news and
gossip—including political news, in which ladies
of the period were not supposed to take an interest, though Mary was always actively involved in

her husband's career. They discussed financial matters, because Lincoln had a horror of debt and wanted to make sure his wife had enough money. Frequently they inquired about each other's health. Both could be mildly flirtatious. Mostly, though, their letters show a warm concern for the well-being of their children.

The oldest of these was Robert Todd Lincoln, born in 1843, mentioned in these family letters as "Bob," or "Bobby." A second son, Edward Baker Lincoln ("Eddy"), was born in 1846. A sickly child, he lived only four years. William Wallace Lincoln ("Willie") was born in 1850 and died in the White House in 1862. The youngest Lincoln, Thomas, was born in 1853 with such a large head and small body that his father said he looked like a tadpole, and he was nearly always called "Tad" or "Taddie." No letters from the three youngest Lincolns to their parents survive, and in the period before 1865 there are only a few from Robert, who left home to study at Phillips Exeter Academy in 1859 and the next year entered Harvard College, from which he graduated in 1864.

The earliest Lincoln family letters date from Lincoln's term in the House of Representatives.

Mary Lincoln, together with Bob and Eddy, accompanied her husband to Washington in December 1847, where the family lived in the boardinghouse of Mrs. Ann G. Sprigg, near the Capitol, but in the spring she took the boys to stay with her father, Robert S. Todd, in Lexington, Kentucky. She never got along with her stepmother, and her letters suggest fairly tense relations in the Todd household. Lincoln's letters to her make it clear that he greatly missed his family.

ABRAHAM LINCOLN TO
MARY TODD LINCOLN

Washington, April 16— 1848—
Dear Mary:

In this troublesome world, we are never quite sattisfied. When you were here, I thought you hindered me some in attending to business; but now, having nothing but business—no variety—it has grown exceedingly tasteless to me. I hate to sit down and direct documents,[1] and I hate to stay in this old room by myself. You know I told you in last sunday's letter, I was going to make a little speech

" . . . I HATE TO STAY IN THIS OLD ROOM BY MYSELF." LETTER TO MARY
TODD LINCOLN FROM ABRAHAM LINCOLN, APRIL 16, 1848

46

during the week; but the week has passed away without my getting a chance to do so; and now my interest in the subject has passed away too. Your second and third letters have been received since I wrote before. Dear Eddy thinks father is "gone tapila[.]"[2] Has any further discovery been made as to the breaking into your grand-mother's house? If I were she, I would not remain there alone. You mention that your uncle John Parker is likely to be at Lexington. Dont forget to present him my very kindest regards.

I went yesterday to hunt the little plaid stockings, as you wished; but found that McKnight has quit business, and Allen had not a single pair of the description you give, and only one plaid pair of any sort that I thought would fit "Eddy's dear little feet." I have a notion to make another trial to-morrow morning. If I could get them, I have an excellent chance of sending them. Mr. Warrick Tunstall, of St. Louis is here. He is to leave early this week, and to go by Lexington. He says he knows you, and will call to see you; and he voluntarily asked, if I had not some package to send to you.

I wish you to enjoy yourself in every possible way;

but is there no danger of wounding the feelings of your good father, by being so openly intimate with the Wickliffe family?[3]

Mrs. Broome has not removed yet; but she thinks of doing so tomorrow. All the house—or rather, all with whom you were on decided good terms—send their love to you. The others say nothing.

Very soon after you went away, I got what I think a very pretty set of shirt-bosom studs— modest little ones, jet, set in gold, only costing 50 cents a piece, or 1.50 for the whole.

Suppose you do not prefix the "Hon" to the address on your letters to me any more. I like the letters very much, but I would rather they should not have that upon them. It is not necessary, as I suppose you have thought, to have them to come free.

And you are entirely free from head-ache? That is good—good—considering it is the first spring you have been free from it since we were acquainted. I am afraid you will get so well, and fat, and young, as to be wanting to marry again. Tell Louisa I want her to watch you a little for me. Get weighed, and write me how much you weigh.

I did not get rid of the impression of that foolish dream about dear Bobby till I got your letter writ-

ten the same day. What did he and Eddy think of the little letters father sent them? Dont let the blessed fellows forget father.

A day or two ago Mr. Strong, here in Congress, said to me that Matilda would visit here within two or three weeks.[4] *Suppose you write her a letter, and enclose it in one of mine; and if she comes I will deliver it to her, and if she does not, I will send it to her.*

Most affectionately

A. Lincoln

MARY TODD LINCOLN TO

ABRAHAM LINCOLN

Lexington May—48—

My dear Husband—

You will think indeed, that old age, *has set* its seal, *upon my humble self, that in few or none of my letters, I can remember the day of the month, I must confess it as one of my peculiarities; I feel wearied & tired enough to know, that this is* Saturday night, *our* babies *are asleep, and as Aunt Maria B[ullock] is coming in for me tomorrow*

49

"I FEEL WEARIED & TIRED . . ., OUR <u>BABIES</u> ARE ASLEEP."
LETTER TO ABRAHAM LINCOLN FROM MARY TODD LINCOLN, MAY 1848

morning, *I think the chances will be rather dull
that I should answer your last letter tomorrow—
I have just received a letter from Frances W*[*al-
lace*],⁵ *it related in an* especial *manner to* THE
BOX *I had desired her to send, she thinks with you
(as good persons generally agree) that it would cost
more than it would come to, and it might be lost on
the road, I rather expect she has examined the speci-
fied articles, and thinks as* Levi⁶ *says, they are* hard
bargains—*But it takes so many changes to do
children, particularly in summer, that I thought it
might save me a few stitches—I think I will write
her a few lines this evening, directing her, not to
send them—She says Willie is just recovering from
another spell of sickness, Mary or none of them were
well⁷—Springfield she reports as dull as usual.
Uncle S*[*amuel Todd*]⁸ *was to leave there on yesterday for Ky—Our little Eddy, has recovered from
his little spell of sickness—Dear boy, I must tell you
a story about him—Bobby in his wanderings to day,
came across in a yard, a little kitten,* your hobby,
*he says he asked a man for it, he brought it trium-
phantly to the house, so soon as Eddy, spied it—his*
tenderness, *broke forth, he made them bring it*
water, *fed it with bread himself, with his* own dear

51

hands, *he was a delighted little creature over it, in the midst of his happiness Ma came in, she you must know dislikes the whole cat race, I thought in a very unfeeling manner, she ordered the servant near, to throw it out, which, of* course, *was done, Ed-screaming & protesting loudly against the proceeding,* she *never appeared to mind his screams, which were long & loud, I assure you—Tis unusual for her* now a days, *to do any thing quite so striking, she is very obliging & accommodating, but if she thought any of us, were on her hands again, I believe she would be* worse *than ever—In the next moment she appeared in a good humor, I know she did not intend to offend me. By the way, she has just sent me up a glass of ice cream, for which this warm evening, I am duly grateful. The country is so delightful I am going to spend two or three weeks out there, it will doubtless benefit the children—Grandma⁹ has received a letter from Uncle James Parker of Miss[ouri] saying he & his family would be up by the twenty fifth of June, would remain here some little time & go on to Philadelphia to take their oldest daughter there to school, I believe it would be a good chance for me to pack up & accompany them —You know I am so fond of* sightseeing *, & I did* not get to *New York or Boston, or travel the lake route—But perhaps, dear husband, like the* irresistible Col Mc,[10] *cannot do without his wife next winter, and must needs take her with him again—I expect you would cry aloud against it—How much, I wish instead of writing, we were together this evening, I feel very sad away from you—Ma & myself rode out to Mr. Bell's splendid place this afternoon, to return a call, the house and grounds are magnificent, Frances W. would* have died *over their rare exotics—It is growing late, these summer eves are short, I expect my long* scrawls, *for truly such they are, weary you greatly—if you come on, in July or August* I *will take you to the springs—* Patty Webb's *school in S[helbyville] closes the first of July, I expect* Mr Webb,[11] *will come on for her. I must go down about that time & carry on quite a flirtation, you know* we, *always had a* penchant *that way. With love* [both words crossed through] *I must bid you good night—Do not fear the children, have forgotten you, I was only jesting —Even E[ddy's] eyes brighten at the mention of your name—My love to all—*

Truly yours

M L—

ABRAHAM LINCOLN TO
MARY TODD LINCOLN

Washington, May 24—1848

My dear wife:

Enclosed is the draft as I promised you in my let-
ter of sunday. It is drawn in favor of your father,
and I doubt not, he will give you the money for it at
once. I write this letter in the post-office, surrounded
by men and noise, which, together with the fact that
there is nothing new, makes me write so short a
letter.

Affectionately

A. Lincoln

ABRAHAM LINCOLN TO
MARY TODD LINCOLN

Washington, June 12. 1848—

My dear wife:

On my return from Philadelphia, yesterday,
where, in my anxiety I had been led to attend the
whig convention[12] I found your last letter. I was so

tired and sleepy, having ridden all night, that I
could not answer it till to-day; and now I have to
do so in the H[ouse]. [of] R[epresentatives]. The
leading matter in your letter, is your wish to return
to this side of the Mountains. Will you be a good
girl in all things, if I consent? Then come along,
and that as soon as possible. Having got the idea in
my head, I shall be impatient till I see you. You will
not have money enough to bring you; but I presume
your uncle will supply you, and I will refund him
here. By the way you do not mention whether you
have received the fifty dollars I sent you. I do not
much fear but that you got it; because the want of it
would have induced you [to?] say something in
relation to it. If your uncle is already at Lexington,
you might induce him to start on earlier than the
first of July; he could stay in Kentucky longer on his
return, and so make up for lost time. Since I began
this letter, the H.R. has passed a resolution for
adjourning on the 17th. July, which probably will
pass the Senate. I hope this letter will not be dis-
agreeable to you; which, together with the circumstances under which I write, I hope will excuse me
for not writing a longer one. Come on just as soon
as you can. I want to see you, and our dear—dear

boys very much. Every body here wants to see our dear Bobby.

Affectionately

A. Lincoln

Washington, July 2. 1848.

My dear wife:

Your letter of last sunday came last night. On that day (sunday) I wrote the principal part of a letter to you, but did not finish it, or send it till tuesday, when I had provided a draft for $100 which I sent in it. It is now probable that on that day (tuesday) you started to Shelbyville; so that when the money reaches Lexington, you will not be there. Before leaving, did you make any provision about letters that might come to Lexington for you? Write me whether you got the draft, if you shall not have already done so, when this reaches you. Give my kindest regards to your uncle John, and all the family. Thinking of them reminds me that I saw your acquaintance, Newton, of Arkansas,[13] at the

Philadelphia Convention. We had but a single interview, and that was so brief, and in so great a multitude of strange faces, that I am quite sure I should not recognize him, if I were to meet him again. He was a sort of Trinity, three in one, having the right, in his own person, to cast the three votes of Arkansas. Two or three days ago I sent your uncle John, and a few of our other friends each a copy of the speech I mentioned in my last letter; but I did not send any to you, thinking you would be on the road here, before it would reach you. I send you one now. Last wednesday, P. H. Hood & Co, dunned me for a little bill of $5.38 cents, and Walter Harper & Co, another for $8.50 cents, for goods which they say you bought. I hesitated to pay them, because my recollection is that you told me when you went away, there was nothing left unpaid. Mention in your next letter whether they are right.

Mrs. Richardson is still here; and what is more, has a baby—so Richardson[14] says, and he ought to know. I believe Mary Hewett has left here and gone to Boston. I met her on the street about fifteen or twenty days ago, and she told me she was going soon. I have seen nothing of her since.

*The music in the Capitol grounds on saturdays,
or, rather, the interest in it, is dwindling down to
nothing. Yesterday evening the attendance was
rather thin. Our two girls, whom you remember
seeing first at Carusis,*[15] *at the exhibition of the
Ethiopian Serenaders, and whose peculiarities were
the wearing of black fur bonnets and never being
seen in close company with other ladies, were at the
music yesterday. One of them was attended by their
brother, and the other had a member of Congress in
tow. He went home with her; and if I were to
guess, I would say, he went away a somewhat
altered man—most likely in his pockets, and in
some other particular. The fellow looked conscious of
guilt, although I believe he was unconscious that
every body around knew who it was that had caught
him.*

*I have had no letter from home, since I wrote you
before, except short business letters, which have no
interest for you.*

*By the way, you do not intend to do without a
girl, because the one you had has left you? Get another as soon as you can to take charge of the dear
codgers. Father expected to see you all sooner; but let*

it pass; stay as long as you please, and come when
you please. Kiss and love the dear rascals.
   Affectionately

A. Lincoln

After the Lincolns returned to Springfield there was little reason for them to correspond with each other, and only two letters suggest how Lincoln's strenuous political career affected his family. The first, written shortly after his enormously success-full Cooper Union address in New York City, recounts his visit to New England, where he saw Robert and his schoolmates at the Phillips Exeter Academy. The second, written shortly after Lincoln was elected President, suggests Robert's decidedly ambivalent feelings about his father's new prominence.

Exeter, N. H. March 4. 1860

Dear Wife:

When I wrote you before I was just starting on a little speech-making tour, taking the boys[16] with me. On Thursday they went with me to Concord, where I spoke in day-light, and back to Manchester where I spoke at night. Friday we came down to Lawrence—the place of the Pemberton Mill tragedy[17]— where we remained four hours awaiting the train back to Exeter. When it came, we went upon it to Exeter where the boys got off, and I went on to Dover and spoke there Friday evening. Saturday I came back to Exeter, reaching here about noon, and finding the boys all right, having caught up with their lessons. Bob had a letter from you saying Willie and Taddy were very sick the Saturday night after I left. Having no despatch from you, and having one from Springfield, of Wednesday, from Mr. Fitzhugh,[18] saying nothing about our family, I trust the dear little fellows are well again.

This is Sunday morning; and according to Bob's orders, I am to go to church once to-day. Tomorrow I bid farewell to the boys, go to Hartford, Conn. and speak there in the evening; Tuesday at Meriden, Wednesday at New-Haven—and Thursday at Woonsocket R. I. Then I start home, and think I will not stop. I may be delayed in New-York City an hour or two. I have been unable to escape this toil. If I had foreseen it I think I would not have come East at all. The speech at New-York, being within my calculation before I started, went off passably well, and gave me no trouble whatever. The difficulty was to make nine others, before reading audiences, who have already seen all my ideas in print.

If the trains do not lie over Sunday, of which I do not know, I hope to be home to-morrow week. Once started I shall come as quick as possible.

Kiss the dear boys for Father.

Affectionately
A. Lincoln

Phillips Exeter Academy
Dec 2d 1860

Dear Mother—

You see I am back at Exeter and I feel very much at home.

I am here with Dick Meconkey. We have been in a constant round of dissipation since we came. On Thursday we were at dinner at Miss Gale's. On Friday Mr Tuck[19] gave a large party, which passed off very finely. Mr. T. thinks of going to Chicago in about three weeks and thence to St. Louis. So look out for him.

Tonight we are invited out to tea which will wind up our fun, as we have to commence study again tomorrow.

We have only about six weeks more before going home.

I see by the papers that you have been to Chicago.

Aint you beginning to get a little tired of this constant uproar?

I have a couple of friends from St. Louis who are going to the inauguration after vacation is over and I have invited them to stop at our house on their road. They are nice fellows and have been with me for the last year.

You will remember I wrote to Father about a fellow who is boring me considerably.

He capped the climax lately. There was a Republican levee and supper at Cambridge to which I was invited. I did not go, for I anticipated what really happened

I was sitting in my room about 9½ and [crossed out] when two boys came up and handed me an admission ticket on the back of which this fellow had written asking me to come over as they were calling for me. I wrote him excusing myself. He must be the biggest fool in the world not to know that I did not want to go over, when if I did, I would be expected to make a speech! Just phancy my phelinks mounted on the rostrum, holding "a vast sea of human faces" &c. I stop overwhelmed.

Yours affectionately
R. T. Lincoln

There is another large gap in the Lincoln family correspondence for the months after his inauguration. During the first year of the presidency, both the Lincolns spent most of the time in the White House. In subsequent years they stayed during the summer months at the Soldiers' Home, a cool retreat three miles north of Washington. Mrs. Lincoln traveled a good deal, at first to Philadelphia and New York, where she bought furnishings to redecorate the White House, and later to New England in order to escape the heat in the White Mountains. Sometimes Tad accompanied her, but at other times he remained with his father. Robert was at Harvard, but he frequently visited his parents in Washington and saw his mother in the mountains. The President, burdened with the management of the huge war effort, had little time to write personal letters; he was, as Mrs. Lincoln noted, "not *given* to letter writing." During the war years he and his wife communicated mostly through telegrams sent by the War Department telegraphic office. Because the Lincolns knew that these despatches were read by telegraphers at each end of the line, they were more restrained and less personal than their earlier letters.

ROBERT T. LINCOLN TO

ABRAHAM LINCOLN

Cambridge
July 17, 1861

A Lincoln

I have the mumps. Home in a few days. Not sick at all   *R T Lincoln*

MARY TODD LINCOLN TO

ROBERT T. LINCOLN

Through War Department Jany 7th 1862

Robert T. Lincoln

Cambridge Mass-

Have you received the passes, sent to you a week since—From Boston to Washington? Return answer, through War Department answer immediately

         Mrs A. Lincoln

By order of President through War Department

[*New York*]
Nov 2d [*1862*]

My Dear Husband—

*I have waited in vain to hear from you, yet as
you are not* given *to letter writing, will be charita-
ble enough to impute your silence, to the right cause.
Strangers come up from W- & tell me you are well
—which satisfies me very much—Your name is on
every lip and many prayers and good wishes are
hourly sent up, for your welfare—and McClellan[20]
& his slowness are as vehemently discussed. Allow-
ing this beautiful weather, to pass away, is dis-
heartening the North—*

*Dear little Taddie is well and enjoying himself
very much—Gen and Mrs Anderson[21] & myself
called on yesterday to see Gen Scott[22]—He looks
well, although complaining of Rheumatism. A day
or two since, I had one of my severe attacks, if it
had not been for Lizzie Keckley,[23] I do not know
what I should have* done*—Some of* these periods,
will launch me away—All the distinguished in the

land, have tried how polite & attentive, they could be to me, since I came up here—Many say, they would almost worship you, if you would put a fighting General, in the place of McClellan. This would be splendid weather, for an engagement. I have had two suits of clothes made for Taddie which will come to 26 dollars—Have to get some fur outside wrappings for the coachman's carriage trappings. Lizze [sic] Keckley, wants me to loan her thirty dollars—so I will have to ask for a check, of $100- which will soon be made use of, for these articles—I must send you, Taddie's tooth—I want to leave here for Boston, on Thursday & if you will send the check by Tuesday, will be much obliged—

One line, to say that we are occasionally remembered will be gratefully received by yours very truly

M. L.

I enclose you a note from Mr Stewart,[24] he appears very solicitous about his young friend. Mr S. is so strong a Union man—& asks so few favors—if it came in your way, perhaps it would not be amiss to oblige—

[*New York, November 3, 1862*]

My dear Husband—

I wrote you on yesterday, yet omitted a very important item. Elizabeth Keckley, who is with me and is working for the Contraband Association,[25] *at Wash is authorized by the* White *part of the concern by a written document—to collect any thing for them—here that, she can—She has been very unsuccessful—She says the immense number of Contrabands in W- are suffering intensely, many without bed covering & having to use any bits of carpeting to cover themselves—Many dying of want—Out of the $1000 fund deposited with you by Gen [Michael?] Corcoran, I have given her the privilege of investing $200 her[e] in bed covering. She is the most deeply grateful being, I ever saw, & this sum, I am sure, you will not object to being used in this way—The cause of humanity requires it— and there will be $800 left of the fund—I am sure, this will meet your approbation—The soldiers are*

well supplied with comfort. Please send check for
$200 out of the fund—she will bring you on the bill

With much love

Yours &

Please write by return mail

[On envelope] *Please answer by return*
mail & send c—

ABRAHAM LINCOLN TO

MARY TODD LINCOLN

Washington,
Nov. 9. 1862

Mrs. A. Lincoln
Boston, Mass.

Mrs. Cuthbert & Aunt Mary²⁶ want to move to
the White House, because it has grown so cold at
Soldiers Home. Shall they?

A. Lincoln

ABRAHAM LINCOLN TO

MARY TODD LINCOLN

Executive Mansion,

Washington, June 9. 1863.

Mrs. Lincoln

Philadelphia, Pa.

Think you better put "Tad's" pistol away. I had an ugly dream about him.

A. Lincoln

ABRAHAM LINCOLN TO

MARY TODD LINCOLN

Executive Mansion,

Washington, June 11, 1863.

Mrs. Lincoln

Philadelphia

Your three despatches received. I am very well; and am glad to know that you & "Tad" are so.

A. Lincoln

ABRAHAM LINCOLN TO

MARY TODD LINCOLN

June 15, 1863.

Mrs. Lincoln
Philadelphia, Pa.
    Tolerably well. Have not rode out much yet, but have at last got new tires on the carriage wheels, & perhaps, shall ride out soon.

A. Lincoln

ABRAHAM LINCOLN TO

MARY TODD LINCOLN

Washington City, D.C.
June 16. 1863

Mrs. Lincoln
Philadelphia.
    It is a matter of choice with yourself whether you come home. There is no reason why you should not, that did not exist when you went away. As bearing

on the question of your coming home, I do not think the raid into Pennsylvania²⁷ amounts to anything at all

A. Lincoln

ABRAHAM LINCOLN TO

ROBERT T. LINCOLN

Executive Mansion,
Washington, July 3rd. 1863.
Robert T. Lincoln, Esq.
Cambridge, Mass.
*Dont be uneasy. Your mother very slightly hurt by her fall.*²⁸

A. L.

Please send at once

ABRAHAM LINCOLN TO

ROBERT T. LINCOLN

Executive Mansion,
Washington, July 11 1863.

R. T. Lincoln
New-York Fifth Ave. Hotel
Come to Washington

A. Lincoln

ABRAHAM LINCOLN TO

ROBERT T. LINCOLN

Washington, D.C.,
July 14 1863

Robt. T. Lincoln
New-York. 5th Av. Hotel–
Why do I hear no more of you?

A. Lincoln

Washington,
July 28 1863

Mrs. A. Lincoln
New-York
  *Bob went to Fort-Monroe & only got back to-
day. Will start to you at 11. AM to-morrow. All
well*

A. Lincoln

ABRAHAM LINCOLN TO

MARY TODD LINCOLN

Executive Mansion,
Washington, August 8, 1863.

My dear Wife.
  *All as well as usual, and no particular trouble
any way. I put the money into the Treasury at five
per cent, with the previlege of withdrawing it any
time upon thirty days' notice. I suppose you are glad*

to learn this. Tell dear Tad, poor "Nanny Goat,"
is lost;[29] and Mrs. Cuthbert & I are in distress
about it. The day you left Nanny was found resting
herself, and chewing her little cud, on the middle of
Tad's bed. But now she's gone! The gardener kept
complaining that she destroyed the flowers, till it
was concluded to bring her down to the White
House. This was done, and the second day she had
disappeared, and has not been heard of since. This is
the last we know of poor "Nanny"

The weather continues dry, and excessively
warm here.

Nothing very important occurring. The election
in Kentucky has gone very strongly right. Old Mr.
Wickliffe got ugly, as you know, ran for Governor,
and is terribly beaten. Upon Mr. Crittendens death,
Brutus Clay, Cassius' brother, was put on the track
for Congress, and is largely elected. Mr. Menzies,
who, as we thought, behaved very badly last session
of Congress, is largely beaten in the District oppo-
site Cincinnati, by Green Clay Smith, Cassius
Clay's nephew.[30] But enough.

Affectionately

A. Lincoln

ABRAHAM LINCOLN TO

MARY TODD LINCOLN

Executive Mansion,

Washington D.C. Aug. 29, 1863

Mrs. A. Lincoln.

Manchester, N. H.

All quite well. Fort-Sumpter[31] *is certainly battered down, and utterly useless to the enemy, and it is believed here, but not entirely certain, that both Sumpter and Fort-Wagner, are occupied by our forces. It is also certain that Gen. Gilmore has thrown some shot into the City of Charleston.*

A. Lincoln

ABRAHAM LINCOLN TO

MARY TODD LINCOLN

Washington, D.C.

Sept. 3. 1863.

Mrs. A. Lincoln

Manchester, Vermont.

The Secretary of War tells me he has telegraphed

Gen. Doubleday[32] *to await further orders. We are all well, and have nothing new.*

A. Lincoln

ABRAHAM LINCOLN TO

MARY TODD LINCOLN

Washington, D.C.,

Sep. 6.1863

Mrs. A. Lincoln
Manchester, Vermont
  All well, and no news, except that Gen. Burn-side has Knoxville, Tennessee.[33]

A. Lincoln

ABRAHAM LINCOLN TO

MARY TODD LINCOLN

Washington, D.C.,

Sep. 20 1863

Mrs. A. Lincoln
New-York
  I neither see nor hear anything of sickness here

now; though there may be much without my know-
ing it. I wish you to stay, or come just as is most
agreeable to yourself.

A. Lincoln.

ABRAHAM LINCOLN TO

MARY TODD LINCOLN

Washington, D.C.,
Sept. 21. 1863

Mrs. A Lincoln
Fifth Avenue Hotel New-York
   The air is so clear and cool, and apparantly
healthy, that I would be glad for you to come.
Nothing very particular, but I would be glad [to]
see you and Tad.

A Lincoln

Executive Mansion, Washington,
Sep. 22, 1863.

Mrs. A. Lincoln
Fifth Avenue House New-York

Did you receive my despatch of yesterday? Mrs.
Cuthbert did not correctly understand me. I directed
her to tell you to use your own pleasure whether to
stay or come; and I did not say it is sickly & that
you should on no account come. So far as I see or
know, it was never healthier, and I really wish to
see you. Answer this on receipt.

A Lincoln

MARY TODD LINCOLN TO

ABRAHAM LINCOLN

New York
September 22, 1863.

A. Lincoln:

Your telegram received. Did you not receive my

reply [?] I have telegraphed Col. McCullum[34] *to*
have the car ready at the earliest possible moment.
Have a very bad cold and am anxious to return
home as you may suppose. Taddie is well.

Mrs. Lincoln.

ABRAHAM LINCOLN TO

MARY TODD LINCOLN

Washington, D.C.,
Sep. 24 1863

Mrs. A. Lincoln,
Fifth Avenue Hotel New York—
    We now have a tolerably accurate summing up of
the late battle between Rosecrans and Bragg.[35] *The*
result is that we are worsted, if at all, only in the
fact that we, after the main fighting was over,
yielded the ground, thus leaving considerable of our
artillery and wounded to fall into the enemies'
hands, for which we got nothing in turn. We lost,
in general officers, one killed, and three or four
wounded, all Brigadiers; while according to rebel
accounts, which we have, they lost six killed, and
eight wounded. Of the killed, one Major Genl. and

80

five Brigadiers, including your brother-in-law, Helm;[36] *and of the wounded, three Major Generals, and five Brigadiers. This list may be reduced two in number, by correction of confusion in names. At 11/40 A.M. yesterday Gen. Rosecrans tele-graph[ed] from Chattanooga "We hold this point, and I can not be dislodged, except by very superior numbers, and after a great battle" A despatch leaving there after night yesterday says, "No fight to-day"*

A. Lincoln.

MARY TODD LINCOLN TO

ABRAHAM LINCOLN

War Dept.
Nov 18th 63

Hon A. Lincoln
Gettysburg, Pa.
   The Dr has just left. We hope dear Taddie is slightly better[37] *will send you a telegram in the morning.*

Mrs Lincoln

MARY TODD LINCOLN TO

ABRAHAM LINCOLN

New York
December 4, 1863

Abraham Lincoln
President United States.
Reached here last evening. Very tired and severe headache. Hope to hear you are doing well. Expect a telegraph to-day.

Mrs. Lincoln

ABRAHAM LINCOLN TO

MARY TODD LINCOLN

Executive Mansion,
Washington, Dec. 4. 9½ AM, 1863

Mrs. A. Lincoln.
Metropolitan, N.Y.
All going well.

A Lincoln

ABRAHAM LINCOLN TO

MARY TODD LINCOLN

Executive Mansion, Washington,

Dec. 5. 10 A.M. 1863

Mrs. A. Lincoln

Metropolitan Hotel, New-[York]

All doing well

A. Lincoln

MARY TODD LINCOLN TO

ABRAHAM LINCOLN

December 6, 1863

A. Lincoln

Do let me know immediately how Taddie and
yourself are. I will be home by Tuesday without
fail; sooner if needed.

Mrs. Lincoln

ABRAHAM LINCOLN TO

MARY TODD LINCOLN

Executive Mansion, Washington, DC

Dec. 6, 1863

Mrs. A. Lincoln.

Metropolitan Hotel N. Y.

All doing well

A. Lincoln

ABRAHAM LINCOLN TO

MARY TODD LINCOLN

Executive Mansion, Washington,

Dec. 7. 10/20 AM. 1863.

Mrs. A. Lincoln

Metropolitan Hotel, N.Y.

*All doing well. Tad confidently expects you
to-night. When will you come?*

A. Lincoln

MARY TODD LINCOLN TO
ABRAHAM LINCOLN

New York
December 7, 1863

A. Lincoln

*Will leave here positively at 8 a.m. Tuesday
morning. Have carriage waiting at depot in Washington at 6 p.m. Did Tad receive his book.*[38]
Please answer.

Mrs. Lincoln

ABRAHAM LINCOLN TO
MARY TODD LINCOLN

Executive Mansion, Washington,
Dec. 7. 7 P.M. 1863

Mrs. A. Lincoln
Metropolitan Hotel N. Y.

*Tad has received his book. The carriage shall be
ready at 6. PM. tomorrow.*

A. Lincoln

ABRAHAM LINCOLN TO

MARY TODD LINCOLN

Washington, D. C.
Jany. 5. 1864
Mrs. A Lincoln—Continental Hotel.
Philadelphia, Pa.
All very well.

A. Lincoln

ABRAHAM LINCOLN TO

MARY TODD LINCOLN

Executive Mansion,
Washington, Jan. 7, 1864.
Mrs. A. Lincoln
Philadelphia, Pa.
We are all well, and have not been otherwise.

A. Lincoln

ABRAHAM LINCOLN TO

ROBERT T. LINCOLN

Executive Mansion,
Washington, Jany. 11 1864.

R. T. Lincoln.
Cambridge, Mass.
  I send your draft to-day. How are you now?
Answer by telegraph at once.

                              A. Lincoln.

ABRAHAM LINCOLN TO

ROBERT T. LINCOLN

Executive Mansion,
Washington, January 19, 1864.

R.T. Lincoln
Cambridge, Mass:
  There is a good deal of small-pox here. Your

friends must judge for themselves whether they
ought to come or not.

A. Lincoln.

Major Eckert:
Please send Above dispatch. Jno. G. Nicolay.[39]

New York City
April 28, 1864

Hon. A. Lincoln
President United States
We reached here in safety. Hope you are well.
Please send me by mail to-day a check for $50
directed to me, care Mr Warren Leland, Metro-
politan Hotel,[40] *Tad says are the goats well?*

Mrs Lincoln

ABRAHAM LINCOLN TO

MARY TODD LINCOLN

Executive Mansion,
Washington,
April 28. 1864.

Mrs. A. Lincoln
Metropolitan Hotel
New-York
The draft will go to you. Tell Tad the goats and
father are very well—especially the goats.

A. Lincoln

ABRAHAM LINCOLN TO

ROBERT T. LINCOLN

Executive Mansion,
Washington, June 14, 1864.

My dear Son
Of course I will try to give the sittings for the
"Crayon."[41]

Your Father
A. Lincoln

ABRAHAM LINCOLN TO

MARY TODD LINCOLN

Executive Mansion, Washington,
June 19, 1864.

Mrs. A. Lincoln,
Fifth Avenue Hotel N.Y.
    Tad arrived safely, and all well.

                    A. Lincoln

ABRAHAM LINCOLN TO

MARY TODD LINCOLN

Executive Mansion,
Washington, June 24, 1864.

Mrs. A. Lincoln
Boston, Mass.
    All well, and very warm. Tad and I have been to
Gen. Grant's army.[42] *Returned yesterday safe and*
sound.

                    A. Lincoln

90

ABRAHAM LINCOLN TO

MARY TODD LINCOLN

Washington, D.C.
June 29. 1864

Mrs. A Lincoln
New-York
All well. Tom⁴³ is moving things out.

A. Lincoln

MARY TODD LINCOLN TO

ROBERT T. LINCOLN

Executive Mansion
Through War Department July 29th [1864]
Mr Robert T. Lincoln
Union Hotel
Saratoga New York—
It is very warm & dusty here. If agreeable to
you, remain a week or ten days longer—on Monday
will send you what is necessary.

Mrs Lincoln

91

ABRAHAM LINCOLN TO

MARY TODD LINCOLN

Office U.S. Military Telegraph,
War Department,
Washington, D.C., August 31. 1864.
Mrs. A. Lincoln.
Manchester, Vermont.
All reasonably well. Bob not here yet. How is
dear Tad?

A. Lincoln

ABRAHAM LINCOLN TO

MARY TODD LINCOLN

Executive Mansion, Washington,
September 8. 1864.

Mrs. A. Lincoln
Manchester, Vermont
All well, including Tad's pony and the goats.
Mrs. Col. Dimmick[44] died night before last. Bob

left Sunday afternoon. Said he did not know
whether he should see you.

A. Lincoln

Office U.S Military Telegraph,
War Department,
Washington, D.C., Sep. 11 1864.

Mrs. A. Lincoln.
New-York.
  All well. What day will you be home? Four
days ago sent despatch to Manchester Vt. for you.

A. Lincoln

ABRAHAM LINCOLN TO
ROBERT T. LINCOLN

Office U.S. Military Telegraph,
War Department,
Washington, D.C., Oct. 11 1864.
Robert T. Lincoln
Cambridge, Mass.
Your letter makes us a little uneasy about your health. Telegraph us how you are. If you think it would help you make us a visit.

A. Lincoln

ABRAHAM LINCOLN TO
MARY TODD LINCOLN

Washington
Dec. 21. 1864

Mrs A Lincoln
Continental Hotel
Do not come on the night train. It is too cold. Come in the morning.

A. Lincoln
Please send above and oblige the President.

John Hay[45]

94

By early 1865 it was clear that the war was near an end, and both the President and Mrs. Lincoln wanted to witness the final Union victory. They now had a strong personal interest in the military operations because on February 1 Robert, despite the strenuous objections of his mother, accepted a commission as captain, assigned to General Grant's staff. In March, realizing that the President was tired out after the second inauguration, Grant invited him and Mrs. Lincoln to visit the army headquarters. Sailing down the Potomac on the *River Queen*, the presidential party reached City Point on March 25. Robert was assigned to escort the distinguished guests. Their stay was not a happy one. Suffering from one of her migraine headaches, Mrs. Lincoln became hysterically jealous of her husband's supposed attention to another woman and created an embarrassing scene. On April 1, to Lincoln's undoubted relief, she went back to Washington, leaving Tad with his father.

When she recovered from her bout of paranoia, Mary Lincoln was overjoyed to learn from her husband of the fall of Petersburg, and she decided to return to the army with a small party of guests.

Just before she left Washington on the uncomfortable *Monohassett*, she heard that Secretary of State William H. Seward had been seriously injured in a carriage accident, and she feared that her husband might rush back to the capital before she reached City Point. He did not do so, but she was disappointed to learn that in her absence he and Tad had visited Richmond. The next day she and her guests boarded the *River Queen* to get their own view of the recently evacuated Confederate capital.

MARY TODD LINCOLN TO

ROBERT T. LINCOLN

Feb. 28, 1865

Capt. Robert T. Lincoln
on Gen Grant's Staff
Gen Grant's Head Quarters
  A message from your Father, will be sent you
tomorrow, I have been ill or would have written
All well now

Mrs Lincoln

ROBERT T. LINCOLN TO

ABRAHAM LINCOLN

Fort Monroe, Va., M[ar]ch 21, 1865
Hon A. Lincoln President, U.S.
   Will you visit the Army this week? Answer at
City Point.

R. T. Lincoln

ABRAHAM LINCOLN TO

ROBERT T. LINCOLN

Cipher   *Office U.S. Military Telegraph,*
                              War Department,
              Washington, D.C., March 21 1865
Capt. R. T. Lincoln
City-Point, Va
   We now think of starting to you about
One P.M. Thursday. Dont make public.

A. Lincoln

Head Quarters Armies of the United States,
City-Point,
April 2. 7/45 [A.M] 1865

Mrs. A. Lincoln,
Washington, D. C.

Last night Gen. Grant telegraphed that Sheridan[46] with his Cavalry and the 5th. Corps had captured three brigades of Infantry, a train of wagons, and several batteries, prisoners amounting to several thousands.[47] This morning Gen. Grant, having ordered an attack along the whole line telegraphs as follows[48]

"Both Wright and Parke got through the enemies lines. The battle now rages furiously. Sheridan with his Cavalry, the 5th. Corps, & Miles Division of the 2nd. Corps,[49] which was sent to him since 1. this A.M. is now sweeping down from the West. All now looks highly favorable. Ord[50] is engaged, but I have not yet heard the result in his front"

Robert yesterday wrote a little cheerful note to
Capt. Penrose,[51] *which is all I have heard of him*
since you left. Copy to Secretary of War

A Lincoln

MARY TODD LINCOLN TO

ABRAHAM LINCOLN

Executive Mansion
Washington
April 2nd [1865]

A Lincoln
City Point
    Arrived here safely this morning, found all well
—Miss, Taddie & yourself very much—perhaps,
may return with a little party on Wednesday—
Give me all the news

Mary Lincoln

ABRAHAM LINCOLN TO
MARY TODD LINCOLN

City Point, Va., April 2, 1865.

Mrs. Lincoln:

At 4:30 p. m. to-day General Grant telegraphs that he has Petersburg completely enveloped from river below to river above, and has captured, since he started last Wednesday, about 12,000 prisoners and 50 guns. He suggests that I shall go out and see him in the morning, which I think I will do. Tad and I are both well, and will be glad to see you and your party here at the time you name.

A. Lincoln.

ROBERT T. LINCOLN TO
ABRAHAM LINCOLN

Hancock Station, April 3rd, 1865

A Lincoln
Prest on Special Train Pitkin
I am awaiting you at Hancock Station

R. T. Lincoln

4 *April 1865*

A. Lincoln
City Point
    Glorious news! Please say to Captain Bradford
[*of the* River Queen] *that a party of seven persons,*
leave here tomorrow & will reach City Point, on
Thursday morning for breakfast—
                              Mrs Lincoln

Fortress Monroe
April 6 [*1865*]
4 o'clock Thursday morning

A. Lincoln
    If Mr Seward, is not too dangerously injured[52]
cannot you remain at City Point until we reach
there at twelve noon to day. We have several friends

on board & would prefer seeing you & returning on
your boat, we are not comfortable here—

Mary Lincoln

MARY TODD LINCOLN TO

ABRAHAM LINCOLN

Fortress Monroe
Ap[ri]l 6 [1865]
9 a. m.

A. Lincoln—

If you are compelled to return before we see you,
which I shall much regret, cannot you return on
some other vessel, we are most uncomfortable on this
& would like your boat—I know you would agree
with me & we will be with you in six hours + at
City Point.

Mary Lincoln

NOTES

1. Having no secretarial help, Lincoln franked thousands of documents with his own signature and sent them out to his constituents.

2. Probably baby-talk for "gone to the Capitol."

3. Robert S. Todd, Mary Lincoln's father, was a personal and political enemy of Robert Wickliffe, who had married one of his cousins.

4. William Strong, a Democratic congressman from Pennsylvania, was married to Matilda Edwards, daughter of Cyrus Edwards of Alton, Illinois.

5. One of Mary Lincoln's older sisters, Frances Wallace was married to Dr. William S. Wallace, a physician and druggist of Springfield.

6. Levi Todd, Mary Lincoln's brother, who was assistant manager of the Oldham, Todd & Company cotton mills in Kentucky.

7. "Willie" was Frances Wallace's husband, and Mary was her daughter.

8. Samuel Todd, brother of Mary Lincoln's father, who had been captured by the Indians in the War of 1812 and held prisoner for a year.

9. Elizabeth Porter Parker, Mary Lincoln's maternal grandmother.

10. Probably John A. McClernand, a Democratic Representative from Illinois.

11. Edwin B. Webb had been one of Mary's suitors in Springfield, but she turned him down in part because he was a widower with two children. One of them, Patty, was now a schoolteacher.

12. The Whig national convention, which met in Philadelphia, June 7–9, nominated Zachary Taylor for President and Millard Fillmore for Vice President.

13. Thomas Willoughby Newton, a prominent Arkansas Whig, who had served in the House of Representatives.

14. Cornelia Sullivan Richardson was the wife of William Alexander Richardson, a Democratic Congressman from Illinois.

15. Carusis Saloon (i.e., salon), where the Lincolns had attended a performance by the Ethiopian Serenaders, minstrels in blackface, who had recently sung for Queen Victoria and the royal family.

16. Robert and his classmate, George Latham, from Springfield.

17. A disastrous fire destroyed the Pemberton Mill in Lawrence, Massachusetts, on January 10, 1860.

18. Harrison G. Fitzhugh, a Republican from Springfield, Illinois, was a carpenter.

19. Amos Tuck, a prominent New Hampshire lawyer, had been a member of the Republican national convention that nominated Lincoln.

20. General George B. McClellan, commander of the Army of the Potomac, was bitterly criticized for his slowness in the Peninsula campaign and, more recently, for his failure to follow up on his victory at Antietam.

21. Robert and Elizabeth Clinch Anderson. Anderson was in command at Fort Sumter when the Confederates attacked in 1861 and afterwards helped in keeping his native state of Kentucky in the Union.

22. Now seventy-six years old, Winfield Scott, after a distinguished career in the Mexican War, was Lincoln's principal military adviser during the early months of the Civil War. He retired in October 1861 on account of his infirmities.

23. Elizabeth Keckley, a mulatto dressmaker who had bought her own freedom, became one of Mary Lincoln's closest confidants.

24. Alexander T. Stewart, owner of the finest drygoods emporium in New York, to whom Mary Lincoln was probably in debt. His note dealt with an army promotion.

25. In the summer of 1862 Mrs. Keckley had been instrumental in organizing the Contraband Relief Organization, to assist the thousands of African-Americans who had fled from the slaveholding states to Washington and other cities in the North. Benjamin F. Butler had applied the term "contraband of war" to these fugitives, in an attempt to offer a legal justification for offering them freedom.

26. Mary Ann Cuthbert was seamstress and later stewardess at the White House, and "Aunt Mary" Dines was a black nurse employed by the Lincolns.

27. The Confederate Army of Northern Virginia had begun crossing the Potomac in a campaign that resulted in the battle of Gettysburg, but at this time Union authorities were not sure that it was more than a raid.

28. On July 22, while driving in from the Soldier's Home to the White House, Mrs. Lincoln had a serious carriage accident.

29. Learning how much the Lincoln boys loved animals, friends gave them two goats, which were named Nanko and Nanny.

30. Charles A. Wickliffe, the candidate of the Peace Democrats, was overwhelmingly defeated by T. E. Bramlett, who supported the Lincoln administration. John J. Crittenden, the former senator, died during the campaign for Congress. Brutus J. Clay, the brother of Cassius M. Clay, Lincoln's minister to Russia, took his place; he was opposed to the policy of emancipation, as was John W. Menzies.

31. Fort Sumter and Fort Wagner guarded the entrance to the Charleston harbor. After both naval and land attacks failed to reduce the forts General Quincy Adams Gillmore undertook formal siege operations, during which Federal artillery reduced Fort Sumter to rubble, but the Confederate garrison continued to hold out. Confederates evacuated Fort Wagner on September 6–7. Though Charleston received some damage from the artillery bombardment, it remained in Confederate hands until the end of the war.

32. Dissatisfied with the performance of General Abner Doubleday during the battle of Gettysburg, General Gorge Gordon Meade removed him from command. Apparently Mrs. Lincoln attempted to intercede with Secretary of War Edwin M. Stanton in Doubleday's behalf, but Doubleday was not returned to duty until December 1863, when he was not given active duty but was assigned to serve on court-martials and commissions.

33. On September 2, Federal troops under General Ambrose P. Burnside entered Knoxville, effectively cutting the last direct railroad link between Richmond and Chattanooga.

34. Daniel C. McCallum, Director of Military Railroads.

35. Either Lincoln's report from the battle of Chattanooga (September 19–20) was incomplete or he was shielding his wife from the bad news. In two days of fierce fighting, the Confederate Army of Tennessee under General Braxton Bragg drove the Federal Army of the Cumberland commanded by General William S. Rosecrans back into the city. Only the indomitable defensive battle waged by General George H. Thomas prevented the Union retreat from becoming a rout.

36. Benjamin Hardin Helm, who married Emily Todd, Mrs. Lincoln's half-sister.

37. Tad was suffering from a severe case of scarlatina. Remembering the deaths of Eddy and Willie, Mrs. Lincoln strongly opposed her husband's leaving her at this critical time to go to Gettysburg.

38. An unidentified gift book, in which she inserted a card: "Taddie Lincoln from his loving Mother Dec 4th 63."

39. Thomas T. Eckert was chief of the War Department telegraph staff. John G. Nicolay was President Lincoln's private secretary.

40. Leland was manager of the Metropolitan Hotel, where Mrs. Lincoln was staying.

41. The editors of *The Collected Works of Abraham Lincoln* speculate that this obscure reference is to Colonel David H. Strother, who used the pseudonym "Porte Crayon" in his sketches for *Harper's New Monthly Magazine*.

42. On June 20 Lincoln and Tad left Washington to visit Grant's army on the James River.

43. There were three "Toms" in the White House—a furnace man, a doorkeeper, and a watchman. One of them was moving the Lincolns' effects to the Soldiers' Home for the summer.

44. The wife of Justin Dimick, the governor of the Soldiers' Home.

45. John Hay was assistant private secretary to the President.

46. General Philip H. Sheridan.

47. Grant's telegram of April 1 at 9:30 P.M. read: "I have just heard from Sheridan. He has carried everything before him . . . he has captured three brigades of infantry and a train of wagons and is now pushing up his success. . . . Several batteries were captured. The prisoners captured will amount to several thousand."

48. Grant's telegram was dated 6:40 A.M., April 2.

49. Generals Horatio G. Wright and John G. Parke of the Fifth Corps, and General Nelson A. Miles of the Second Corps.

50. General Edward O. C. Ord, who commanded the Army of the James.

51. Captain Charles B. Penrose had been detailed by the Secretary of War to accompany the President on his visit to the army.

52. Secretary of State William H. Seward suffered a broken jaw and arm in a carriage accident on April 5.

David Herbert Donald is a Charles Warren Professor of American History and Professor of American Civilization Emeritus at Harvard University. Many of his books deal with American history during the Civil War era: *Lincoln's Herndon* (1948); (with others) *Divided We Fought: A Pictorial History of the War, 1861-1865* (1952); *Inside Lincoln's Cabinet: The Civil War Diaries of Salmon P. Chase* (1954); *Lincoln Reconsidered: Essays on the Civil War Era* (1956); *Charles Sumner and the Coming of the Civil War* (Pulitzer Prize in biography, 1960); (with J. G. Randall) *The Civil War and Reconstruction* (1961); (with others) *The Great Republic: A History of the American People; Charles Sumner and the Rights of Man* (1970); *Look Homeward: A Life of Thomas Wolfe* (Pulitzer Prize in biography, 1987); and *Lincoln* (Lincoln Prize, 1995).